Babies Do Come
with a Manual

Babies Do Come with a Manual

Nancy French

Deb Habenicht

Jayne Sconzert

BROWN BOOKS
PUBLISHING GROUP

Babies Do Come with a Manual

Brown Books Publishing Group
16250 Knoll Trail Drive, Suite 205
Dallas, Texas 75248
www.BrownBooks.com
(972) 381-0009

A New Era in Publishing™

ISBN 978-1-61254-212-6
Library of Congress Control Number 2015943705

Printed in the United States
10 9 8 7 6 5 4 3 2 1

For more information or to contact the authors, please go to www.BabiesDoComeWithAManual.com

This manual is dedicated to our children, Douglass, Bradley, Alice, Daniel, Tim, Megan, and Mallory, who may someday have children, and to all people who are parents, who will be parents, and who are caregivers.

Contents

NOTE TO THE READER

In explaining the various skills and processes, we chose to write in a gender-neutral style whenever possible. When such gender-neutral wording proved awkward, we opted for male gender references, instead of a mix between masculine and feminine ones, for the sake of consistency.

Introduction

As occupational, speech, and physical therapists, we have noticed for years the gradual decline of physical fitness, strength, coordination, and communication skills not only in our patients but in the general population. As a result of these skill deficits, children are often not ready for kindergarten. Kindergarten teachers frequently report that their students have difficulties with gross and fine motor skills, sustained attention, fatigue, and social skills. This has weighed heavily on our hearts. We have become passionate about educating parents, teachers, and caregivers. This book was written to empower people to change that trend, starting with their own families.

Currently, children's developmental milestones are delayed as compared to before 1992. We have found, on average, babies are rolling over, sitting unsupported, crawling, and walking several months later than documented prior to 1992.

Repeatedly putting your child in positioning devices—such as infant carriers that transition into car seats, strollers, and floor positioners—can limit your child's ability to move freely. This can cause your child's head to become misshapen (plagiocephaly) and delay motor movements.

Too often, children play with toys and electronic devices that foster little imagination and require few motor skills. Children are often playing games on computers, tablets, or smartphones that have exciting and stimulating graphics. This instant gratification can limit creativity and encourage impulsivity. Instead of using their imaginations, drawing from memory and experience, children only need to click a button to view or create an image.

Although in today's society we have cutting-edge technology to help with every aspect of our lives, raising healthy children in modern society is *not easy*. These modern conveniences that appear to make our lives simpler are, in fact, adversely affecting the growth and development of our children. In general, our children's gross and fine motor skills are delayed, visual attention is reduced, and sensory experiences and social interactions are limited. This has created a generation of children who are often not ready for kindergarten, much less the world, as they mature into adults.

Exposing your child to technology (screen time) too early can be harmful, affecting your child's ability to focus and socialize. Too much technology too early can, later in life, create addictive behavior, a sedentary lifestyle, social isolation, and continual distraction.

There should be no screen time (including tablets, computers, smartphones, and other video electronics) until age two. Babies need "real" experiences, not virtual replacements. Do not give your child your smartphone/tablet for entertainment; you will thank us later. Babies learn from you, not technology.

The American Academy of Pediatrics recommends that babies sleep on their backs until they can roll over themselves. Because babies are sleeping all night long on their backs, placing them on their tummies during awake hours is very important. The recommended tummy time is three times daily for three to five minutes or as tolerated from birth until they roll over.

This manual provides a simple "how-to" approach for meaningful interaction and effective communication with your child from birth to five years to build strong foundational skills that will provide lifetime benefits.

Each section provides information and simple activities. By following these activities from birth to five years, you'll watch your child develop important language, motor, sensory, visual, cognitive, and social skills. Blank pages are included throughout this handbook for easy note taking and keepsakes. These notes will then be readily available as needed to share with your doctor and child care providers.

Before the developmental guidelines sections, the following information will give a brief overview with definitions of skills and reflexes.

Types of Skills and Their Definitions

What Are Fine Motor Skills?

Fine motor skills utilize the small muscles of your body for precise, coordinated movements, such as grasping a rattle, picking up small objects, feeding, dressing, writing, cutting, coloring, and gluing.

What Are Gross Motor Skills?

Gross motor skills are large muscle movements, such as lifting the head, rolling, propping on elbows, maintaining hands and knees position, crawling, walking, running, hopping, jumping, and skipping.

What Are Communication Skills?

Communication skills include the ability to convey and exchange information, ideas, feelings, attitudes, intentions, and perceptions. Verbal communication involves language, articulation, voice, and fluency skills.

- Language Skills: Language skills are made up of social rules that include word meanings, making new words, combining words together, using grammar and syntax rules, and using language socially to communicate.
- Articulation Skills: How speech sounds are produced and the intelligibility of sounds.
- Voice Skills: These skills are characterized by vocal quality, pitch, loudness, resonance, and duration, as appropriate for an individual's sex and age.
- Fluency Skills: The flow, rate, and rhythm of oral speech.

What Are Visual Motor Skills?

The area of visual motor skills is the ability to coordinate visual information with motor movements of the eyes and body, such as visual tracking, reaching and grasping for objects, drawing, writing, and all eye-hand coordination activities. This area is broken down into several eye movements, including saccade, smooth pursuit, and focal point.

The eye movement of saccade is visually scanning your environment at various points, stopping at each point and perceiving what you see correctly. This visual skill is used when scanning text, playing games such as tag, and in most sports. Smooth pursuit is visually scanning your environment without stopping, giving your brain constant feedback. Focal point is looking at an object and focusing for periods of time, like watching a movie.

Another important visual skill is viewing your environment through the periphery of your vision. This allows you to not only see what is in front of you, but to the side as well. This skill is extremely important for safety and general awareness of your total surroundings.

These visual skills cannot be developed from a computer screen. They develop from a variety of real-life visual experiences.

What Is Sensory Processing?

Sensory processing is the process of organizing all sensory input (auditory, tactile, visual, taste, and smell) to enable you to perform all of your daily activities effectively.

- Auditory Processing: The area of auditory processing includes hearing and interpreting sounds in your environment and is vital to enabling you to interact appropriately with your environment. This sense determines how you interact during learning and play and helps to keep you safe in your surroundings. Some children have difficulties in this area, either being too sensitive (over-reactive) or not sensitive enough (under-reactive). Both can cause problems in the school and home environments.

- Tactile (touch) Processing: The area of tactile (touch) processing is the sense that tells your brain the texture, temperature, and amount of pressure you are using to touch an object. This is an extremely important sense for safety and daily interaction with your environment. This sense is developed over time through interaction with various tactile media and experiences. Without these experiences, this system can become either hyperresponsive or hyporesponsive to tactile experiences and cause problems with daily activities.

- Visual Perception Processing: The area of visual processing includes but is not limited to acuity and perception. Visual processing is much more than seeing your environment clearly for near and far distance. Visual perception helps you navigate through your daily life efficiently.

Visual perception is made up of depth, figure-ground, visual discrimination, visual closure, and form constancy.

— Depth perception is how you see and perceive your environment in three dimensions. This enables you to judge distance and grasp objects effectively. This sense helps you navigate appropriately through space, part of spatial orientation. Without this skill, riding a bike, playing on equipment, or driving a car would be next to impossible to do safely.

— The perceptual skill of figure-ground is finding items in competing backgrounds. This is important for locating needed items in your environment, completing worksheets in school, and keeping materials organized in general.

— The sense of visual discrimination is noticing details in objects/designs and how they are different. This is an important skill that enables us to discriminate our environment.

— The sense of visual closure helps us perceive what an object would be when completed. For example, when viewing a picture or letter that is partially drawn, being able to visually complete the picture/letter in your brain is critical. This is an important skill in drawing and printing letters.

— Finally, the sense of form constancy is the visual-perceptual skill of realizing that a form/shape is the same whether it is smaller/larger or darker/lighter. This skill helps as well with drawing and writing letters and is developed over time with repeated exposure to a variety of real-life visual experiences.

● Taste Processing: The sense of taste includes perceiving flavors and textures of food. This is a basic survival sense, and it is very important for obtaining proper nutrition. Children need to experience a wide variety of healthy foods in a fun, encouraging manner. If your child is given mainly healthy food from the moment he is fed, then that is what he will acquire a taste for in the future. A child can't crave foods he hasn't eaten.

Make sure you are modeling good eating habits and providing healthy, nutritious food for proper development. Family meals are extremely important for modeling eating nutritious food, as well as for socializing with your family when seated at the table. Don't underestimate the power of eating all together at the table during the busy week.

- Smell Processing: The sense of smell is an extremely powerful sense, influencing memory and emotion. It is more sensitive than any other sensory system. Aroma therapy can be a powerful tool. There are scents that increase concentration, such as orange, lemon, eucalyptus, and rosemary. There are scents that increase confidence, such as rose, jasmine, and sage. Sandalwood, orange, and vanilla scents can be used to encourage relaxation and reduce stress.

Children can be over-responsive and under-responsive to smells. Both of these sensory deficits cause problems for children. If children are over-responsive, they can overreact to ordinary odors, avoiding areas with offensive odors, such as bathrooms, kitchens, and lunchrooms. Children may even be bothered by perfume worn by teachers. This may manifest in undesirable behaviors, such as not wanting to complete work, avoiding group activities, and not entering certain public areas. The sense of smell is often overlooked as a catalyst for bad behavior. Children who are under-responsive to smell may not smell important odors such as smoke, gas, or even rotten food. Be aware of potential difficulties in this area, and adjust your child's environments when necessary to avoid long-term impact.

Types of Reflexes and Their Definitions

What Are Newborn Reflexes?

Babies are born with automatic, involuntary movements (reflexes) that assist in their survival. These movements begin around the twenty-fifth week of pregnancy and will typically fade away as babies learn to move and protect themselves by their first birthday. Without proper positioning of the infant, these reflexes may not fade away by their first birthday, which can interfere with normal development of movement.

Some of the newborn reflexes are: Moro, ATNR, STNR, Rooting, Sucking, Stepping, TLR, Grasping, and Galant.

- The *Moro Reflex* protects the baby from loud noises. It involves the baby moving his head away from the sound, spreading his hands, and extending his arms. It is important for protection of the baby. It is present at birth and fades at about two months.

- The *Asymmetrical Tonic Neck Reflex* (ATNR) helps the baby to roll over. It typically disappears at the time the *Symmetrical Tonic Neck Reflex* (STNR) evolves. STNR assists the baby in crawling and maintaining hands and knees (rock & roll) positioning.

- The *Rooting Reflex* helps the newborn find the breast or bottle, and the *Sucking Reflex* helps the baby coordinate suck/swallow. Both of these reflexes go away between one to two months.

- The *Stepping Reflex* is present from birth to two months. It is very important for development of walking posture.

- The *Tonic Labyrinthine Reflex* (TLR) is present from birth to about four months. This reflex is important for developing muscle tone, balance, and posture. These skills will be needed later in life for coordination, spatial awareness, and vision, as well as attention to task.

- The *Grasping Reflex* arrives around birth and helps the baby develop grasp patterns. It usually goes away by six months.

- The *Galant Reflex* helps the baby to roll from the tummy to the back. It fades away around five to six months. The Galant Reflex assists the baby in moving down the birth canal, and it is responsible for sitting balance and development of bladder control.

Reflexes that appear at the end of the first year of life include the *Protective Extension*, *Flexor Withdraw*, and *Deep Tendon Reflexes*. These reflexes provide the baby with protection in sitting and stance.

Nutrition

For your child to grow properly, he needs not only to be nurtured physically and socially, but to eat healthy food. In America today, foods are highly processed, containing excessive amounts of salt, sugar, and preservatives. Consumers have to hunt for foods that are not highly processed. Our children's diets are limited—that is, fewer are eating family meals and more are relying on fast food—and contain many more additives and preservatives than years ago. Children's bodies need good fuel to sustain focus throughout the day. Many children are not eating enough protein on a regular basis. Protein is needed for brain and skeletal muscle development. Kids' school snacks are often chips or processed snack foods, which contain carbohydrates, too much salt and sugar, and no protein. These snacks do not support brain health or help in supporting sustained attention throughout the school day. Give your children the gift of a healthy diet so that they can make better choices regarding food and nutrition later in life.

Simple Guidelines for Mealtime

These tips should help your child expand his diet and may help him in avoiding becoming a "picky eater."

- Most eating and drinking should be done at the table.
- Create family-style meals: one menu for the entire family.
- Offer healthy foods over and over so your child gets used to seeing, smelling, and tasting these foods.
- Encourage your child to be involved with meal preparation and selection. There are many children's cookbooks that can make mealtime healthy and fun.
- Limit snacks before dinner so that your child is hungry at mealtime.
- Reduce the overall refined sugar and preservatives in your child's diet. Read nutrition labels.

Please know that these tips and suggestions provide only some basic guidelines for healthy and improved nutrition.

It's Playtime

Playtime is critical to your child's overall development. Children learn to communicate, to develop social skills, to take turns, and to follow rules/directions. Children also develop important fine and gross motor skills during play. Play is your child's occupation and the primary avenue of learning.

Human interaction, like peekaboo, songs we sing, and words we coo to our infants, creates early connections to critical thinking that cannot be substituted for with CDs or language DVDs.

"Giving your child attention helps build their brain because the brain is sculpted through experience," states Dr. Sandra Bond Chapman, founder and chief director of the Center for Brain Health at the University of Texas at Dallas.

In *Brain Rules for Baby*, John Medina points out, "The greatest pediatric brain-boosting technology in the world is a plain cardboard box, a fresh box of crayons, and 2 hours! The worst: a flat screen television, computer, video games." Medina goes on to argue that language DVDs may actually reduce vocabulary when presented to your infant. The number and type of words you use when talking to your infant can improve IQ and vocabulary, but they must come from you.

Rebel Play Group: Be a rebel; host a technology-free play group. Gather activities and games that address all of the foundational skills, including gross motor, fine motor, communication, self-care, sensory, and social skills. Look for games/activities that are low tech and that require social interaction and imagination. Simple activities are best. Research "old-fashioned" games/activities; these will be new and exciting for you and your child and will foster healthy development. Be the first in your neighborhood to host this "new-style" play group and begin to spread the word through your community. We want your child's future to be healthy and bright. Get outside and play.

Developmental Guidelines

These developmental stages are basic guidelines. Your child will develop at his own rate. It is acceptable if your child develops several months slower or faster than these guidelines. Always share any concerns with your doctor.

NOTES

Normal Development at
ONE MONTH

Fine Motor
— Holds hands in tight fists when resting on back

Visual Motor
— Notices and shows interest in black-and-white or high-contrast patterns
— Enjoys interaction with human faces
— Acknowledges stationary objects

Gross Motor
— Holds head up at times while on tummy

Reflexes
Moro, ATNR, Rooting, Suck/Swallow, TLR, Palmar and Plantar Reflexes, Galant, Stepping

Communication

— Listens to the rhythm and melodies of speech
— Usually can pick out his mother's voice
— Child uses undifferentiated crying, which is crying that sounds the same and does not really vary by specific needs

Playtime Activities

Tummy time: The American Academy of Pediatrics recommends positioning your infant on his tummy three times a day for three to five minutes during awake time.

Reminder . . . no screen time for your baby, and have daily tummy time.

● Each day, talk, sing, rock, and hold your baby; you cannot do this too much.

Reason: Your baby needs social and sensory experiences. This is your baby's main avenue of learning, growing, and developing properly.

● Look into his eyes.

Reason: Prolonged eye gaze and joint attention are very important nonverbal communication skills.

● When you hear your child "coo," coo back. Say something. Talk. Sing.

Reason: This lets your child know you are listening.

● Make sure you do not leave your baby in one position too long (carrier, swing, bed).

Reason: To prevent malformation of the head and provide a better visual and sensory experience, it's important to change the baby's position throughout the day.

● Place your baby on his tummy on a flat (not fiber-filled) blanket or a firm, supported surface. When his head is lifted above the ground, gently turn his head from side to side while calling his name or shaking a toy above his head.

Reason: Promotes head turning when baby is on his tummy; encourages listening and looking.

- While your baby is lying on his back or in a baby carrier, place your index finger in each of his hands. After he grasps your fingers, gently lift him so that he is bearing some weight on his fingers.

  Reason: Promotes grasping and head control.

- Shake rattle while holding it approximately twelve inches from his nose for five seconds.

  Reason: Promotes development of visual motor skills.

- Provide high-contrast (black-and-white) toys, such as mobiles, books, etc.

  Reason: Promotes visual perception skills.

NOTES

Normal Development at
TWO MONTHS

Fine Motor

— Opens and shuts hands

Visual Motor

— Focuses visually on objects six inches away
— Becomes active when a toy is seen
— Responds with a smile
— Looks into caregiver's face and eyes with interest

Gross Motor

— Elevates head and upper trunk forty-five degrees, bears weight on forearms, and grasps rattle

Reflexes

Moro, ATNR, Rooting, Suck/Swallow, TLR, Palmar and Plantar Reflexes, Galant, Stepping

Communication

— May startle when hearing loud sounds
— Sucking behavior changes in response to sound
— Often quiets or smiles when spoken to
— Makes pleasure sounds, like cooing

Playtime Activities

Reminder . . . no screen time for your baby, and have daily tummy time.

- Each day, talk, sing, rock, and hold your baby; you cannot do this too much.

  Reason: Your baby needs social and sensory experiences. This is your baby's main avenue of learning, growing, and developing properly.

- Make sure you do not leave your baby in one position too long (carrier, swing, bed).

  Reason: To prevent malformation of the head and provide a better visual and sensory experience, it's important to change the baby's position throughout the day.

- Your baby needs a lot of social interaction. Talk to him.

  Reason: This is how he learns to communicate and bond with his family.

- Place your baby on a flat blanket (not fiber-filled) on the floor on his tummy and hold a mirror, rattle, or toy while gently rubbing along the side of his back.

  Reason: Promotes social interaction and visual attention and helps integrate the Galant Reflex.

- Place rattle in his hand and shake gently. He should drop the rattle after about five seconds.

  Reason: Promotes proper grasping.

- While on his tummy, place pull toy about six inches in front of him. Move toy from left to right and encourage him to follow it visually.

  Reason: Encourages visual tracking and expansion of visual field.

NOTES

Normal Development at
THREE MONTHS

Fine Motor
— Grasps rattle placed in hand
— Brings hands to mouth
— Bats at objects

Visual Motor
— Reacts when your face disappears from view
— Looks at feet and hands
— Sees objects at a distance of twelve inches
— While on back, eyes follow back and forth

Gross Motor
— Head trails body a bit when being pulled up from lying into sitting position
— Rests on forearms while on tummy, with head at ninety degrees

Reflexes

Moro, Rooting, Suck/Swallow, and Stepping are integrated, ATNR begins to integrate, TLR, Palmar and Plantar Reflexes, Galant

Communication

— Begins to recognize familiar voices and will often quiet if crying
— Begins to cry differently for different needs
— Begins to smile when he sees you

Playtime Activities

Reminder . . . no screen time for your baby, and have daily tummy time.

● Each day, talk, sing, rock, and hold your baby; you cannot do this too much.

  Reason: Your baby needs social and sensory experiences. This is your baby's main avenue of learning, growing, and developing properly.

● Make sure you do not leave your baby in one position too long (carrier, swing, bed).

  Reason: To prevent malformation of the head and provide a better visual and sensory experience, it's important to change the baby's position throughout the day.

● Instead of picking him up, slowly lift your baby to sitting using his hands, allowing time for his head to adjust.

  Reason: Encourages head, neck, and trunk control.

● Place him under suspended toys/mobile that he can bat with his hands. Guide his arm if necessary. DO NOT PLACE AN ELECTRONIC TABLET IN THE CRIB OR SUSPENDED ABOVE YOUR BABY.

Reason: Promotes coordination of the visual motor skills of reaching and grasping three-dimensional objects.

- Play peekaboo with your child; place brightly colored ankle and wrist toys on him and gently shake his hands and feet.

  Reason: Promotes social interaction, visual attention, purposeful movement, and object permanence.

- Play with him by holding him in different positions (tilting side to side or backward).

  Reason: Helps develop sense of balance.

NOTES

Normal Development at
FOUR MONTHS

Fine Motor

— Holds breast/bottle with one or both hands
— Reaches/engages hands together while lying on back
— Clutches at objects
— Grasps and holds a cube
— Can hold a toy and shake it and swing at dangling toys
— Brings hands to mouth

Visual Motor

— Initiates smiling, smiles spontaneously at people
— Eyes track objects
— Copies some facial expressions (smiling, frowning)

Gross Motor

— Pushes up with hands while on tummy
— Rolls from back to left or right with opposite arm crossing over

— Holds head steady, unsupported
— Pushes down with legs when feet are on a hard surface

Reflexes

Moro, Rooting, Suck/Swallow integrates, ATNR continues
to integrate, STNR emerges, TLR begins to integrate, Palmar
and Plantar Reflexes begin to integrate, Galant begins
to integrate

Communication

— Starts to move eyes in direction of sound
— Begins to respond to different changes in the tone of your
  voice
— Begins babbling and cooing using different sounds in
  response to your voice

Playtime Activities

Reminder . . . no screen time for your baby, and have daily
tummy time.

● Each day, talk, sing, rock, and hold your baby; you
  cannot do this too much.

  Reason: Your baby needs social and sensory experiences. This is your baby's main avenue of learning, growing,
  and developing properly.

● Make sure you do not leave your baby in one position
  too long (carrier, swing, bed).

  Reason: To prevent malformation of the head and provide a better visual and sensory experience, it's important to change the baby's position throughout the day.

● Place him on his back with a toy to one side. Roll him by
  his hips to the side by the toy.

  Reason: Assists in rolling over and reaching for a toy.

● Place him in supported sitting and play pat-a-cake.

Reason: This helps in learning to imitate motor movements and gain control of his hands. This is also an interactive social experience.

- Suspend a bright toy in front of him and brush the back of his hand with the toy to stimulate reaching. Give him a piece of tissue paper to crumple with both hands, but remove it before he puts it in his mouth.

  Reason: This activity helps develop in-hand manipulation skills, as well as providing a tactile experience.

- Play with him by holding him in different positions (tilting side to side or backward).

  Reason: This helps to develop sense of balance. Balance is an important building block to all motor development.

NOTES

NORMAL DEVELOPMENT AT
FIVE MONTHS

Fine Motor

— Puts fingers into mouth
— Transfers objects (hand-mouth-hand)
— Grasps small objects in palm

Visual Motor

— Looks for dropped objects
— Looks from one to the other of two objects
— Smiles at self in front of mirror
— Turns head past midline

Gross Motor

— Lifts head when pulled to sitting
— Sits with pelvic support
— Protectively extends hands when falling forward

Reflexes

ATNR and TLR continue to integrate, STNR is emerging, Palmar and Plantar Reflexes continue to integrate, Galant

Communication

— Begins to respond to own name
— Notices and enjoys toys that make noise
— Listens to music

Playtime Activities

Reminder . . . no screen time for your baby, and have daily tummy time.

● Each day, talk, sing, rock, and hold your baby; you cannot do this too much.

   Reason: Your baby needs social and sensory experiences. This is your baby's main avenue of learning, growing, and developing properly.

● Make sure you do not leave your baby in one position too long (carrier, swing, bed).

   Reason: To prevent malformation of the head and provide a better visual and sensory experience, it's important to change the baby's position throughout the day.

● Place him on his back with knees bent. Grasp his hands and raise him up to sitting, as if doing a sit-up.

   Reason: This exercise encourages head, neck, and trunk control.

● In supported sitting, place pacifier, cube, or empty spool on table in front of him and encourage him to pick it up. Make sure the toy is not so small that it is a choking hazard.

   Reason: This activity helps develop the eye-hand coordination skill of reaching and grasping.

- Place him in front of a mirror and make silly faces; move mirror to his side.

  Reason: This facilitates turning his head past the middle of his body and encourages social interaction and imitation skills.

- Play with him by holding him in different positions (tilting side to side or backward).

  Reason: This develops sense of balance and spatial orientation.

NOTES

Normal Development at
SIX MONTHS

Fine Motor
— Holds small objects with palm, fingers, and thumb
— Brings a bottle to mouth by self
— Uses raking grasp to obtain objects
— Begins to pass objects from one hand to the other
— Brings toys/food to mouth

Visual Motor
— Has full color vision
— Looks at objects several feet away

Gross Motor
— Begins to sit without support
— Rolls over from tummy or back
— When standing, supports weight on legs and may bounce

Reflexes

ATNR, TLR, Galant, Palmar and Plantar Reflexes are integrated, STNR is emerging, Protective Extension to the front is established in sitting

Communication

— Babbles with many different, playful sounds, including p, b, and m
— Begins to giggle and laugh
— Vocalizes pleasure and displeasure
— Reacts to loud, angry, or friendly voices
— Turns in the direction of new sounds
— Babbles and gurgles for attention

Playtime Activities

Reminder . . . no screen time for your baby, and have daily tummy time.

● Each day, talk, sing, rock, and hold your baby; you cannot do this too much.

   Reason: Your baby needs social and sensory experiences. This is your baby's main avenue of learning, growing, and developing properly.

● Respond to your child's gurgles, babblings, and coos.

   Reason: Treat his babbling/vocalizations as if they were real language. This will let your baby know that you are communicating with him.

● Make sure you do not leave your baby in one position too long (carrier, swing, bed).

   Reason: To prevent malformation of the head and provide a better visual and sensory experience, it's important to change the baby's position throughout the day.

- Place him on the floor in sitting position. Sit behind him, but do not support him. Place small toys between legs and encourage him to reach for them.

  Reason: This activity helps develop reaching, grasping, balance, and trunk control.

- Place him in a high chair or in your lap at a table. Place a cup with handles in front of him and bang it a few times. Encourage him to imitate.

  Reason: This activity encourages social imitation skills and improves reaching and grasping skills.

- Place small bits of preferred pureed food on the high chair tray and encourage him to pick it up, using a raking motion. Encourage finger feeding at this time.

  Reason: This activity improves grasping and hand control.

- Provide colorful toys and activities.

  Reason: This stimulates color vision.

- Play with him by holding him in different positions (tilting side to side or backward).

  Reason: This develops sense of balance.

NOTES

Normal Development at
SEVEN MONTHS

Fine Motor
— Bangs a toy on the floor
— Uses hands and mouth to explore objects
— Pulls round peg out of a pegboard

Visual Motor
— Discriminates circle/square/triangle/cross
— Eyes follow a dropped object (tracking)

Gross Motor
— Commando crawls
— Puts feet to mouth
— Protectively extends from side to side
— Tailor sits (crisscross applesauce sitting) unsupported; DO NOT ALLOW "W-SITTING." "W-sitting" is when children sit with their knees forward and legs tucked behind, forming a W.

— Maintains balance while moving hands and arms outside base of support to grasp a toy; grasps cube with thumb, first, and second fingers

Reflexes

STNR continues to emerge, Protective Extension to the front and side in sitting

Communication

— Hears words as distinct sounds
— Turns to look in the direction of various sounds
— Uses varying sounds to get attention

Playtime Activities

Reminder . . . no screen time for your baby, and have daily tummy time.

● Each day, talk, sing, rock, and hold your baby; you cannot do this too much.

Reason: Your baby needs social and sensory experiences. This is your baby's main avenue of learning, growing, and developing properly.

● Place him on floor in sitting position and allow him to play with plastic containers, pots/pans, and wooden spoons.

Reason: This facilitates wrist rotation, exploration, and balance.

● Encourage toys that pour or turn during play.

Reason: This activity helps teach smooth motor movements and develops fine motor skills.

● Encourage toys that require two hands, such as pop beads, blocks, cymbals, etc.

Reason: This encourages the use of two hands together in a cooperative fashion.

- DO NOT ALLOW "W-SITTING."

  Reason: This position stretches your child's hips, knees, and ankles excessively.

- Place him on the floor on his stomach and present toys that push/pull. Encourage him to push up on his hands with elbows extended.

  Reason: Promotes crawling and visual attention that crosses the midline of his body.

- Begin simple, one- to four-shape puzzles, shape sorters, and pegboards.

  Reason: Develops problem-solving and fine motor skills, utilizing different grasp patterns.

- Play with him by holding him in different positions (tilting side to side or backward).

  Reason: Develops sense of balance and spatial orientation.

NOTES

Normal Development at
EIGHT MONTHS

Fine Motor

— Picks up and holds a small object in each hand

— Holds a pellet between thumb and side of index finger

Visual Motor

— Plays peekaboo

— Pats, smiles at, and tries to kiss self in mirror

Gross Motor

— Independently gets into sitting position

— Reaches with one hand while on hands and knees

Reflexes

STNR, Protective Extension to the front and sides, Protective Extension to the back emerging

Communication

— Responds to own name
— Pats image of self in a mirror
— Produces four or more different sounds
— Listens to his own vocalizations and those of others
— Frequently uses repeated syllable (baba, dada, gaga)

Playtime Activities

Reminder . . . no screen time for your baby, and have daily tummy time.

● Each day, talk, sing, rock, and hold your baby; you cannot do this too much.

  Reason: Your baby needs social and sensory experiences. This is your baby's main avenue of learning, growing, and developing properly.

● Read big, colorful books to your child every day.

  Reason: Reading develops vocabulary.

● Place him on the floor in sitting position, without support. Do not allow "W-sitting." Present toys such as blocks, large pegboards, musical instruments, etc. Place toys to the side and behind him so that he must rotate his trunk to find the toys.

  Reason: This promotes balance and core strengthening.

● Play pat-a-cake, clapping, and peekaboo games in sitting position.

  Reason: This encourages him to cross the middle of his body and promotes social interaction and object permanence.

● Place child on hands and knees and encourage him to rock back and forth.

Reason: This prepares for creeping (a.k.a. crawling).

- Provide him with smaller toys that encourage him to use thumb and side of index finger to grasp objects. Be careful of choking.

  Reason: This develops grasping patterns and in-hand manipulation skills.

- Introduce finger foods, such as ripe bananas, low-sugar cereal, teething crackers, etc.

  Reason: Promotes eye-hand coordination skills, as well as building interest in healthy foods and independent eating.

- Play with him by holding him in different positions (tilting side to side or backward).

  Reason: This develops sense of balance and spatial orientation.

NOTES

Normal Development at
NINE MONTHS

Fine Motor

— Waves bye-bye

— Releases objects intentionally

— Holds object with thumb and finger tips

— Uses fingers to point at things

— Transfers toys from one hand to another

— Grasps pellet with pad of thumb and pad of index finger

Visual Motor

— Realizes objects exist even when not seen, such as food dropped out of sight or a toy put under a blanket (object permanence)

— Looks at pictures in a book after they are named (example: "Look at the cow")

Gross Motor

— Pulls to stand
— Creeps on hands and knees with opposite arm and leg moving together

Reflexes

STNR, all protective reflexes intact (blink, gag, extension, cough, flexor withdraw), more mature reflexes emerging

Communication

— Begins to enjoy simple games like peekaboo and pat-a-cake
— Begins to use simple nonverbal gestures to communicate (holding arms to be picked up, waving, and blowing a kiss)

Playtime Activities

Reminder . . . no screen time for your baby.

- Each day, talk, sing, rock, and hold your baby; you cannot do this too much.

  Reason: Your baby needs social and sensory experiences. This is your baby's main avenue of learning, growing, and developing properly.

- Give him toys that can be squeezed or manipulated other ways with his hands; place small pellets, peas, etc. on the table and have him hand them to you individually, using the thumb and index finger. Always be careful of choking.

  Reason: These activities encourage and develop in-hand manipulation skills and grasp patterns.

- Play "doggie," and have the child imitate you on all fours, creeping. Have him "chase" you.

  Reason: This encourages social interaction and imitation skills and develops imagination skills.

- Bounce him in supported standing, flexing and extending his knees.

  Reason: Promotes strengthening to prepare for walking independently.

- Read simple picture books, pointing to the pictures and naming them.

  Reason: This improves visual attention, concentration, cognitive skills, and social interaction.

- Encourage toys that require releasing an object into a container.

  Reason: Promotes eye-hand coordination and improves in-hand manipulation skills.

- Play with him by holding him in different positions (tilting side to side or backward).

  Reason: This develops sense of balance and spatial orientation.

NOTES

Normal Development at
TEN MONTHS

Fine Motor
— Creeps while holding object in one hand
— Picks up string with thumb and index finger
— Isolates index finger and pokes

Visual Motor
— Looks closely at tiny objects

Gross Motor
— Cruises around furniture
— Walks with two hands held

Reflexes
All primitive reflexes should be integrated. Reflexes will no longer be addressed.

(In research conducted by Jayne Sconzert, PT, eighteen out of twenty-one beginning kindergarten students in one class at a large metropolitan elementary school in Flower Mound, TX, exhibited abnormal ATNR reflex in the school year 2011-2012.)

Communication

— May shout or babble to attract attention

— Uses jargon (babbling that sounds like real speech)

— Says syllables or sequence of sounds repeatedly

Playtime Activities

Reminder . . . no screen time for your baby.

- Each day, talk, sing, rock, and hold your baby; you cannot do this too much.

    Reason: Your baby needs social and sensory experiences. This is your baby's main avenue of learning, growing, and developing properly.

- While sitting or standing, have him pop bubbles with index finger or stomp on them with one foot.

    Reason: Improves finger-isolation skills and develops gross motor coordination skills.

- Place preferred toys around a table and encourage him to sidestep (cruise) around the table to obtain them.

    Reason: Improves balance and develops pre-walking skills.

- Have him turn pages of a thick book, one at a time, while reading a story. Encourage pointing to pictures in the book.

    Reason: Develops visual attention, finger isolation, fine motor skills, and social interaction.

- Play with him by holding him in different positions (tilting side to side or backward).

  Reason: This develops sense of balance and spatial orientation skills.

- Continue to recite songs, finger plays, and nursery rhymes.

  Reason: Child learns that words have meaning with rhythm and sequence.

NOTES

Normal Development at
ELEVEN MONTHS

Fine Motor
— Grasps and pulls strongly with one or both hands
— Tears paper
— Plays with simple musical instruments
— Picks up small objects with the pads of fingers

Visual Motor
— Perfects object permanence
— Visually tracks rolling ball

Gross Motor
— Stands alone
— Walks with one hand held

Communication
— Continues to babble and attempts to say real words
— Imitates lots of different speech sounds

43

Playtime Activities

Reminder . . . no screen time for your baby.

- Each day, talk, sing, rock, and hold your baby; you cannot do this too much.

  Reason: Your baby needs social and sensory experiences. This is your baby's main avenue of learning, growing, and developing properly.

- Place toys on the sofa so that he must pull up to standing to retrieve them.

  Reason: This encourages pulling to stand and improves sustained visual attention.

- Introduce push toys. Always model playing with the newly introduced toy.

  Reason: This encourages independent walking.

- Walk with him holding one or both hands; try to keep his arms down and not over his head.

  Reason: This encourages normal independent walking and improves balance and coordination skills.

- Play with three- to four-piece puzzles of simple shapes; present paper and crayons for scribbling and imitating vertical strokes.

  Reason: This promotes spatial orientation skills and fine motor skills and develops grasp patterns. This also encourages imitation and social interaction.

- Play ball. Sit across from child and roll a six- to eight-inch ball back and forth.

  Reason: This activity improves gross motor skills, visual motor skills, eye-hand coordination skills, and social interaction.

- Practice counting fingers and toes.

  Reason: This encourages vocabulary growth.

- Talk about colors.

  Reason: This encourages descriptive vocabulary growth.

NOTES

Normal Development at
TWELVE MONTHS

Fine Motor

— Grasps thick crayon/pencil in fist
— Turns thick pages one at a time
— Shakes, bangs, and throws toys to explore
— Picks up small objects with finger tips

Visual Motor

— Watches objects he throws
— Walks heel-toe with a reciprocal pattern
— Grasps with the tip of the thumb and index finger
— Picks up two cubes with one hand and holds them

Gross Motor

— Gets into a standing position independently
— May take a few steps independently
— May stand alone for a few seconds

Communication

— Recognizes own name and names of family members
— Points to objects and pictures that you name
— Says at least three words
— Begins to imitate simple words
— Understands very simple instructions
— Uses speech to get and keep attention

Playtime Activities

Reminder . . . no screen time for your baby.

- Provide him with activities using crayons, markers, and finger paint. When he is finger painting, he can use pudding, whipped cream, etc. When bathing him, introduce water play with squirt toys, soap paint, and pouring containers.

    Reason: These activities provide an important, sensory-rich experience, as well as improving fine motor skills.

- While sitting, gently bounce a ball back and forth about five feet.

    Reason: This develops visual and gross motor skills and social interaction.

- Have him squat to pick up toys and put them in the toy box.

    Reason: This activity develops balance and gross motor skills.

- Play in half-kneeling position (kneeling on one knee).

  Reason: This encourages him to transition to standing through half-kneeling.

- Play simple games, music, and finger plays.

  Reason: Child recognizes that words are symbols for objects, wants, and needs.

NOTES

Normal Development at
EIGHTEEN MONTHS

Fine Motor

— Gets spoon in mouth right-side up, little spilling

— Uses one hand more often than the other

— Scribbles spontaneously

— Drinks from a cup

Visual Motor

— Names one body part on self

— Selects and puts square/rectangle into shape sorter

Gross Motor

— Throws ball while standing

— Seats self in small chair

— Walks alone

— May walk up steps

— Pulls/pushes toys while walking
— Can help dress himself

Communication

— Uses at least fifteen to twenty words
— Combines two-word phrases and questions, such as "go bye-bye," "up now," "all gone," "where daddy?"
— Imitates words more accurately
— Points to several basic body parts
— Brings familiar objects from another location when asked
— Follows simple one-step directions
— Can sing or hum simple songs
— Can name at least five objects or pictures
— Makes "sounds" of familiar animals
— Shows a lot of affection toward parents
— Loves to vocalize

Playtime Activities

Reminder . . . no screen time for your child.

• Self-feeding with a spoon, no matter how messy. Play-Doh; coloring, pour-and-spill activities with water, rice, sand, etc. Playing with blocks, building towers, and shape sorters.

  Reason: These activities provide a sensory-rich experience, as well as developing eye-hand coordination skills, self-care skills, fine motor skills, and social interaction.

• "Bear-walking"; bean bag toss from four feet; kicking a ball back and forth from three to four feet; jumping on a trampoline with hands held; tossing an eight-inch ball back and forth from three feet. Begin sitting on small tricycle.

  Reason: These activities improve gross motor coordination skills.

- Read books to your child frequently.

  Reason: Reading increases vocabulary development.

- Look at your child when he talks to you, and respond to your child's attempts to communicate.

  Reason: This encourages reciprocal give-and-take communication with others.

- Talk with your child about what you're doing while on outings, such as taking walks in the neighborhood; going to the park, on a picnic, or to the playground; cleaning house; or watering flowers.

  Reason: Conversation increases vocabulary and concept development.

- Keep your speech simple, in short, three-word sentences.

  Reason: Child will better understand short and simple communication, and it is easier for him to imitate.

NOTES

Normal Development at
TWO YEARS

Fine Motor

— Holds crayon with fingers
— Imitates circular/vertical scribble
— Stacks four- to six-cube tower
— Squeezes/pulls play dough apart
— Names simple objects in bag with eyes closed
— Unbuttons large, easy buttons
— Holds an object with one hand while using the other, such as paper and pencil

Visual Motor

— Identifies six body parts
— Matches primary colors/simple shapes
— Completes a simple three-piece puzzle
— Stacks rings in correct order

Gross Motor

— Jumps in place with both feet together
— Kicks a stationary ball
— Throws overhand

Communication

— Understands simple requests and questions
— Can point to and name most body parts
— Talks with self, dolls, and other toys
— Uses two- to three-word sentences
— Begins to ask simple questions, such as "what's this?" "where's doggie," "why?"
— Begins to use negatives, such as "no go," "not want"
— Has a vocabulary of about two hundred words
— Will ask specifically for things like drink, food, toys, and toilet
— Can stay with an activity for at least five to seven minutes
— Begins to use some plurals by adding "s" (shoes, books, toys)
— Names pictures in a book

Playtime Activities

Reminder . . . no screen time for your child, and host a rebel play group (technology free).

● Pull toys; walking backward; stomping on bubble wrap; marching to music; musical chairs; bean bag or ball toss to a basket/target; begin tricycle training.

Reason: These activities help develop gross motor co-ordination skills as well eye-hand coordination, balance, and weight shift.

● Playing with blocks/cubes (stacking four to six blocks/cubes); begin imitation of vertical stroke and circle with crayons, finger paint, and/or whipped cream; dressing dolls; begin snipping with scissors on index cards.

Reason: These activities encourage coordinated fine motor movements and the use of appropriate pressure for fine motor tasks. Using different media (finger paint, whipped cream, shaving cream) exposes your child to sensory input and helps regulate and develop the senses of touch and smell. Imitating pre-writing strokes helps develop future writing skills and increases visual motor coordination. Dressing and snipping with scissors develop skills that require two hands working together.

- Play "Bean Bag Boogie" (place bean bag on basic body part and name the part); play with puzzles that incorporate matching colors and shapes.

  Reason: These types of games teach spatial awareness, as well as improving and developing cognitive skills.

- Talk about situations before you go, while you're there, and again when you come home.

  Reason: This models correct speech and language for your child.

- Carry on conversations with your child, taking turns and listening to each other.

  Reason: Conversation encourages reciprocal communication with others.

- Have your child finish your sentences by leaving off the last word ("Let's go ride in the <u>car,</u>" "Let's build a tower with your <u>blocks</u>").

  Reason: This gives your child opportunities to use new words.

- Expand what your child is saying (for example, if the child says, "More cracker," the parent should ask, "Tim wants more crackers?").

NOTES

Normal Development at
THREE YEARS

Fine Motor

— Does finger plays while singing songs
— Uses fingers to show age
— Demonstrates hand preference
— Grasps pencil with thumb, finger, and index
— Buttons/unbuttons medium-sized buttons

Visual Motor

— Counts five objects aloud
— Matches block patterns
— Completes a ten-piece, form-board puzzle

Gross Motor

— Walks heel to toe
— Catches large ball

— Rides a tricycle

— Alternates feet when climbing stairs

Communication

— Matches and names most primary colors

— Uses contractions (it's, she's)

— Begins to understand basic spatial concepts (in, on, under)

— Knows name, gender, and age

— Has a vocabulary of nearly one thousand words

— Sentence length is three to four words

— Can consistently produce these sounds: n, m, f, h, b, p, and w

— Enjoys singing songs

— Stays with a single activity for eight to ten minutes

— Asks lots of "wh" questions

— Speech is understood most of the time

— Understands some shapes

Playtime Activities

Reminder . . . allow only one hour of screen time at this age per day, and host a rebel play group (technology free).

● Riding a tricycle; T-ball; batting balloon with preschool-sized racquet; bouncing eight-inch ball back and forth from five feet; stick horse; parachute games; Duck, Duck, Goose; modified kickball; hippity-hop.

Reason: These activities develop eye-hand coordination, gross motor skills, and imagination. These games are also important in developing various social skills, such as turn taking, playing with others, and communicating.

● Where is Thumbkin?; coloring, cutting, gluing; play dough; practice vertical, horizontal, diagonal, and circular lines; clean up own toys; put own dishes in the sink.

Reason: All of these activities develop fine motor, pre-writing, and self-care skills. Playing finger games such as Where is Thumbkin? helps develop finger isolation, which improves hand manipulation skills.

- Encourage buttoning and unbuttoning of his own clothes.

  Reason: Improves self-care skills and use of both hands in a coordinated fashion.

- Continue to expand on your child's communication by providing new and descriptive words.

  Reason: Increases vocabulary and encourages conversation and thinking skills.

- Ask your child to tell you about the day's activities.

  Reason: Summarizing gives your child the opportunity to practice his words while recalling information.

- Ask your child questions that would require a choice instead of "yes" or "no." Example: "Do you want milk or juice?"

  Reason: Increases vocabulary and encourages conversation and thinking skills.

NOTES

Normal Development at
FOUR YEARS

Fine Motor

— Grasps pencil with thumb and fingers
— Touches tip of thumb to each finger
— Moves fingers in fine, localized movements when writing with marker
— Places key in lock
— Cuts on line
— Brushes teeth, combs hair, and dresses with little assistance
— Prints some letters

Visual Motor

— Discriminates size/more and less
— Sorts objects by color/size/shape
— Arranges pictures in correct sequence

Gross Motor

— Runs fluidly

— Hops on one foot

— Gallops

— Can throw, catch, and bounce a ball

Communication

— Points to and names colors

— Points to circles, squares, and triangles

— Follows simple directions even when object is not present

— Asks many questions

— Sentence length is four to five words

— Begins to use more complex sentences

— Begins to use past tense and plurals

— Vocabulary is nearly fifteen hundred words

— Stays with an activity for at least twelve minutes

— Correctly produces the following sounds: n, m, p, f, h, w, k, g, y, d, and t

— Most people understand child's speech

— Answers simple "wh" questions

Playtime Activities

Reminder . . . allow only one hour of screen time at this age per day, and host a rebel play group (technology free).

● Hopscotch; begin jump rope activities; kickball; T-ball; soccer; Velcro toss and catch; two-wheeled scooter; wheelbarrow walks; animal walks.

Reason: These activities develop gross motor coordination, balance, and strengthening. Remember . . . games also encourage social interaction and improve cooperation, following directions, and being connected.

- Using clothespins; puzzles; Play-Doh; color, cut, glue; paper airplanes; books; Legos; cars; dolls; lacing cards; ink stamps. Begin writing letters of the alphabet/name.

  Reason: These are simple, low-tech activities that encourage imagination and improve and develop fine motor and pre-writing skills.

- Encourage independent self-care activities, such as tooth brushing, hair combing, and dressing.

  Reason: These tasks improve self-care skills, teaching and empowering children to help care for themselves.

- Help child to categorize objects and things like transportation, animals, foods, and clothing.

  Reason: Categorizing increases vocabulary skills.

- Talk about how objects/pictures are the same and different.

  Reason: This increases ability to understand how things are related.

NOTES

Normal Development at
FIVE YEARS

Fine Motor

— Laces a card with a running stitch
— Colors within the lines
— Cuts and pastes simple shapes
— Draws a person with five body parts

Visual Motor

— Ties shoes
— Uses a knife to spread things
— Prints own name legibly

Gross Motor

— Independently rides a bike
— Bounces and catches a tennis ball with dominant hand
— Independently walks on a balance beam
— Jumps rope

Communication

— Can identify objects by their functions

— Knows spatial concepts, such as over, under, on, in, behind, far, and near

— Knows the city he lives in

— Sentence length is five to six words

— Uses most speech sounds correctly with the exception of l, th, sh, ch, s, and r, which usually develop later

— Knows some opposites, such as up/down, big/little, happy/sad

— Counts at least five to ten objects

— Can retell a simple story

— Uses past, present, and future tenses when speaking

— Asks many questions

— Stays with one activity for at least thirteen to fifteen minutes

— Identifies numbers and letters

Playtime Activities

Reminder . . . allow only one hour of screen time at this age per day, and host a rebel play group (technology free).

● Family bike rides; tree climbing; hiking up/down hills; walking or riding bike to school; jump rope games; four square; tag; parachute games; hula hoop.

   Reason: These activities foster social skills while developing gross motor coordination. Many of these activities provide a chance to teach your child about the real world around him, instead of looking at a video screen talking about virtual reality.

● Shoe-tying board; board games such as Chutes and Ladders, Candy Land, Twister, Hands Down; activity books; sidewalk chalk; card games.

Reason: These activities provide and develop so many important skills, such as turn taking, fine motor skills, gross motor skills, balance, coordination, and sensory input, and they help increase focus and concentration.

- Encourage drawing a person with five or more body parts, coloring within the lines, cutting, and gluing.

  Reason: These activities encourage kindergarten readiness skills.

- Encourage your child to use language rather than motions and gestures to express ideas, feelings, wants, and needs.

  Reason: This encourages your child to talk, and it stimulates language and social skills growth.

- Read signs to your child when driving in the car or out on walks.

  Reason: Talking teaches the child that words have meaning.

- Have your child help plan activities, such as what you will make for lunch or dinner.

  Reason: This encourages your child to use words and sequence steps.

- Play family card games and board games together.

  Reason: Games develop social skills, back-and-forth conversation, turn-taking skills, waiting, and following rules.

- Play "pretend" games such as "house," "cooking," or "dolls" with your child while exchanging roles in the family.

  Reason: This stimulates imagination and role play.

Conclusion

From birth, babies are placed on their backs in many forms. The use of infant carriers, swings, positioning devices, chairs, and swaddling blankets is causing a lack of human touch due to modern technology. We are not sure what harm these practices will do long term, but we know that lack of human interaction can cause many problems in social, sensory, motor, and cognitive development. We need to recognize this lack of social interaction in our society and get our children back to basics.

DVDs, computer games, and video games are all sedentary activities that may have long-lasting effects when presented too early.

If you have any concerns about your child's development, contact your pediatrician. He or she can recommend appropriate professional evaluations and/or interventions. This may include, but is not limited to, physical, occupational, or speech therapy.

About the Authors

Nancy French, OTR, graduated from Washington University in St. Louis, MO, with her BS in occupational therapy. As a pediatric occupational therapist, she has practiced primarily in school settings, helping students to develop and improve their fine motor, visual motor, bilateral, and self-care skills. She works with children from birth to twenty-one years of age and across all levels of ability and needs. Nancy has extensive experience in the areas of autism and food aversion therapy and has developed professional seminars for both schools and communities. She is married and has three grown children.

Deb Habenicht, MA, CCC-SLP, graduated from Augustana College with a BA and from the University of Illinois with a master's degree in speech/language pathology. Since then, she has worked with hearing-impaired students in Bettendorf, IA, and in the Preschool Language Development Program at the UT Dallas Callier Center for Communication Disorders. Deb works in the public school system with preschool and elementary populations. She currently lives in Highland Village, TX, with her husband. They have two married sons.

Jayne Sconzert graduated from the University of Texas Southwestern Medical Center in 1982 with a bachelor's degree in physical therapy. She worked in neurorehabilitation for five years as a senior physical therapist at the Dallas Rehabilitation Institute, followed by five years at Community Rehab Services as the director of outpatient physical therapy. She has been a pediatric physical therapist in the public school system since January of 1994. Her areas of expertise include neurology, neuroanatomy, power mobility, development, lower-extremity orthotics, and assistive technology.

References

Bowen, C. July 23, 2014. "Typical Speech and Language Acquisition in Infants and Young Children." Accessed July 28, 2014. http://www.Speech-Language-Therapy.com/Index.php?option=com_content&view=article&id=35:admin&catid=2:uncategorised&Itemid=117.

Ernsperger, Lori, and Tania Stegen-Hanson. 2004. *Just Take a Bite: Easy and Effective Answers to Food Aversion and Eating Challenges.* Arlington, TX: Future Horizons Inc.

Fraker, C., L. Walbert, and S. Cox. 2007. *Food Chaining.* New York: De Capo Press.

Herbert, Sonya N. "Baby Talk Builds Brain Blueprint, Strong Relationships." *Dallas Morning News,* March 11, 2011.

Hunter, J., and M. Malloy. March 2002. "Effect of Sleep and Play Positions on Infant Development: Reconciling Developmental Concerns with SIDS Prevention." *Newborn and Infant Nursing Reviews* 2 (1): 9–16.

Janz, J., C. Blosser, and L. Freuchting. June 1997. "A Motor Milestone Change Noted with a Change in Sleep Position." *The Archives of Pediatric Medicine* 151 (6): 565–68.

Johnson, Chris Plauche, and Peter A. Blasco. July 1991. "Infant Growth & Development." *Pediatrics in Review* 18 (7): 224–42.

Kranowitz, Carol. 2006. *Catching Kids Before They Fall.* SensoryWorld.com.

Medina, John. 2008. *Brain Rules for Baby: How to Raise a Smart and Happy Child from Zero to Five.* Seattle, WA: Pear Press.

Moyes, Rebecca. 2010. *Building Sensory Friendly Classrooms.* Arlington, TX: Sensory World.

Rowen, Chris, Andrew Doan, and Hilarie Cagh. "10 Reasons Why Handheld Devices Should Be Banned for Children Under the Age of 12." *Huffington Post*, March 6, 2014. Updated Oct. 1, 2014.

Salls, Joyce, Lyn N. Silverman, and Carolyn M. Gatty. Sept. 2002. "The Relationship of Infant Sleep and Play Positioning to Motor Milestone Achievement." *The American Journal of Occupational Therapy* 56 (5): 577–80.

Wilson-Jones, Martha. Winter 2004. "Supine and Prone Infant Positioning: A Winning Combination." *Journal of Perinatal Education* 13 (1): 10–20.

Young, Charlene. 2012. *Effective Neurological Management of Sensory Processing Disorder.* Cross Country Education Workshop.

USEFUL WEBSITES

- American Speech-Language-Hearing Association:
  www.ASHA.org/Public/Speech/Development
- Beyond Therapy:
  www.CentralFLTherapy.com
- Child Development Institute:
  www.ChildDevelopmentInfo.com
- *Encyclopedia of Children's Health:*
  www.HealthOfChildren.com
- *Medline Plus:*
  www.NLM.NIH.gov/MedlinePlus
- Rhythmic Movement Training International:
  www.RhythmicMovement.com
- Primary Reflexes:
  www.SproutingReflexes.Weebly.com